Contents

Note: Clauses marked* should be completed/deleted as appropriate.

	ARTICLES OF AGREEMENT	*Page 3*
	Recitals (1st to 5th)	4
	Articles	5
1	Contractor's obligations	
2	Contract sum	
3	Architect/Contract Administrator	
4	Planning Supervisor	
5	Principal Contractor	
6	Dispute or difference – adjudication	
7A	Dispute or difference – arbitration	
7B	Dispute or difference – legal proceedings	
7C	Dispute or difference – fallback position	
	Attestation	9

CONDITIONS

1	**Intentions of the parties**	11
1·1	Contractor's obligations	
1·2	Architect's/Contract Administrator's duties	
1·3	Reappointment of Planning Supervisor or Principal Contractor – notification to Contractor	
1·4	Alternative B in the 5th recital – notification by Contractor – regulation 7(5) of the CDM Regulations	
1·5	Giving or service of notices or other documents	
1·6	Reckoning period of days	
1·7	Applicable law	
1·8	Contracts (Rights of Third Parties) Act 1999 – contracting out	
2	**Commencement and completion**	11
2·1*	Commencement and completion	
2·2	Extension of contract period	
2·3*	Damages for non-completion	
2·4	Practical completion	
2·5*	Defects liability	
3	**Control of the Works**	12
3·1	Assignment	
3·2	Sub-contracting	
3·3	Contractor's representative	
3·4	Exclusion from the Works	
3·5	Architect's/Contract Administrator's instructions	
3·6*	Correction of inconsistencies	
3·7*	Variations	
3·8	Provisional sums	
4	**Payment**	13
	(see also clauses 5·2 and 5·3, if applicable)	
4·1	Payments subject to Supplemental Condition C	
4·2*	Progress payments and retention	
4·3*	Penultimate certificate	
4·4	Notices of amounts to be paid and deductions	
4·5*	Final certificate	

4	**Payment** *continued*	
4·6*	Contribution, levy and tax changes	
4·7	Fixed price	
4·8	Right of suspension by Contractor	
5	**Statutory obligations**	15
5·1	Statutory obligations, notices, fees and charges	
5·2*	Value added tax	
5·3	Construction Industry Scheme (CIS)	
5·4	[Number not used]	
5·5	Prevention of corruption	
5·6	Employer's obligation – Planning Supervisor – Principal Contractor	
5·7	Duty of Principal Contractor	
5·8	Successor appointed to the Contractor as the Principal Contractor	
5·9	Health and safety file	
6	**Injury, damage and insurance**	16
6·1	Injury to or death of persons	
6·2*	Injury or damage to property	
6·3A*	Insurance of the Works by Contractor – Fire etc.	
6·3B*	Insurance of the Works and any existing structures by Employer – Fire etc.	
6·4	Evidence of insurance	
7	**Determination**	17
7·1	Notices	
7·2	Determination by Employer	
7·3	Determination by Contractor	
8	**Settlement of disputes**	18
8·1	Adjudication	
8·2	Arbitration	
8·3	Legal proceedings	

SUPPLEMENTAL CONDITIONS

A*	Contribution, levy and tax changes	19
B	Value added tax	21
C	Construction Industry Scheme (CIS)	23
D	Adjudication	24
E	Arbitration	26

	GUIDANCE NOTE	27
	List of amendments incorporated in this reprint	32

MW 98 (9/03) © The Joint Contracts Tribunal Limited 2003

This Agreement

This Agreement is only intended for use where the Client has engaged a professional consultant to advise on and to administer its terms.

is made the _____ day of _____ 20_____

Between

_____

of _____

_____

_____

_____

('the Employer') of the one part

And

_____

of (or whose registered office is at) _____

_____

_____

_____

('the Contractor') of the other part.

Whereas

Recitals

1st the Employer wishes the following work _____

_____

_____

to be carried out under the direction of

_____

(hereinafter called 'the Architect/the Contract Administrator') [a]

and has caused
   drawings numbered _____
   (hereinafter called the 'Contract Drawings') [b]
   and/or a Specification (hereinafter called the 'Contract Specification') [b]
   and/or schedules [b]
   (which documents are together with the Conditions and the Supplemental Conditions
   A to E annexed hereto hereinafter called the 'Contract Documents' [c])
   showing and describing the work
to be prepared and which are attached to this Agreement;

2nd the Contractor has stated the sum he will require for carrying out such work, which sum is that stated in article 2, and has priced the Specification [b] or the schedules [b] or provided a schedule of rates [b];

3rd the Contract Documents have been signed by or on behalf of the parties hereto;

4th [b] the quantity surveyor appointed in connection with this Agreement shall mean

_____

or in the event of his death or ceasing to be the quantity surveyor for this purpose such other person as the Employer nominates for that purpose;

[d] 5th A. [e] All the Construction (Design and Management) Regulations 1994 (the 'CDM Regulations') apply to the work referred to in the 1st recital; and the Employer has instructed the Architect/ the Contract Administrator that the design of the Works is to comply with the provisions of regulation 13 of the CDM Regulations;

B. [e] Regulations 7 and 13 only of the Construction (Design and Management) Regulations 1994 (the 'CDM Regulations') apply to the work referred to in the 1st recital; and the Employer has instructed the Architect/the Contract Administrator that the design of the Works is to comply with the provisions of regulation 13 of the CDM Regulations;

---

[a] Where the person named is entitled to the use of the name 'Architect' under and in accordance with the Architects Act 1997 delete 'the Contract Administrator': in all other cases delete 'the Architect'. Where 'the Architect' is deleted the expression 'the Architect' shall be deemed to have been deleted throughout this Agreement; where 'the Contract Administrator' is deleted the expression 'the Contract Administrator' shall be deemed to have been deleted throughout this Agreement.

[b] Delete as appropriate.

[c] Where a Contract Document has been priced by the Contractor it is this document that should be attached to this Agreement.

[d] Where alternative A applies, see the notes on the JCT 80 Fifth recital in Practice Note 27 'The application of the Construction (Design and Management) Regulations 1994 to Contracts on JCT Standard Forms of Contract' for the statutory obligations which must have been fulfilled before the Contractor can begin carrying out the Works.

[e] Delete whichever of the alternatives A and B is not applicable.

Now it is hereby agreed as follows

Article 1

Contractor's obligations

For the consideration hereinafter mentioned the Contractor will in accordance with the Contract Documents carry out and complete the work referred to in the 1st recital together with any changes made to that work in accordance with this Agreement (hereinafter called the 'Works').

Article 2

Contract sum

The Employer will pay the Contractor for the Works the sum of _____

_____

_____(£_____)

exclusive of VAT or such other sum as shall become payable hereunder at the times and in the manner specified in the Contract Documents.

Article 3

Architect/Contract Administrator

The term 'the Architect/the Contract Administrator' in the said Conditions shall mean

_____

or in the event of his death or ceasing to be the Architect/the Contract Administrator for the purpose of this Agreement such other person as the Employer shall within 14 days of the death or cessation as aforesaid nominate for that purpose, provided that no person subsequently appointed to be the Architect/the Contract Administrator under this Agreement shall be entitled to disregard or overrule any certificate or instruction given by the Architect/the Contract Administrator for the time being.

Article 4 [f]

Planning Supervisor

A. [g] The term the 'Planning Supervisor' in the Conditions shall mean the Architect/the Contract Administrator

B. [g] The term the 'Planning Supervisor' in the Conditions shall mean

_____

of _____

or, in the event of the death of the Planning Supervisor or his ceasing to be the Planning Supervisor, such other person as the Employer shall appoint as the Planning Supervisor pursuant to regulation 6(5) of the CDM Regulations.

---

[f] Delete articles 4 and 5 when alternative A in the 5th recital is deleted.

[g] Delete alternative A or alternative B as appropriate (retaining the final paragraph).

Article 5 [f]

Principal Contractor

The term the 'Principal Contractor' in the Conditions shall mean the Contractor or, in the event of his ceasing to be the Principal Contractor, such other contractor as the Employer shall appoint as the Principal Contractor pursuant to regulation 6(5) of the CDM Regulations.

Article 6

Dispute or difference – adjudication

If any dispute or difference arises under this Agreement either party may refer it to adjudication in accordance with the procedures set out in Supplemental Condition D. If, under clause D2, the parties have not agreed a person as the Adjudicator the nominator of the Adjudicator shall be:

The President or a Vice-President or the Chairman or a Vice-Chairman:
* Royal Institute of British Architects
* The Royal Institution of Chartered Surveyors
* Construction Confederation
* National Specialist Contractors Council Limited

* Delete all but one

(If no nominator is selected the nominator shall be the President or a Vice-President of the Royal Institute of British Architects; if the nominator fails to nominate, the nominator shall be one of the other listed nominators selected by the party requiring the reference to adjudication.)

Article 7A

Dispute or difference – arbitration

[h] Subject to article 6, if any dispute or difference as to any matter or thing of whatsoever nature arising under this Agreement or in connection therewith, except in connection with the enforcement of any decision of an Adjudicator appointed to determine a dispute or difference arising thereunder, shall arise between the parties either during the progress or after the completion or abandonment of the Works or after the determination of the employment of the Contractor, except under Supplemental Condition B clause B6 (*Value added tax*) or under Supplemental Condition C (*Construction Industry Scheme*) to the extent provided in clause C14, it shall be referred to arbitration in accordance with the procedures set out in Supplemental Condition E.

If, under clause E2·1, the parties have not agreed a person as the Arbitrator the appointor of the Arbitrator shall be:

The President or a Vice-President:
* Royal Institute of British Architects
* The Royal Institution of Chartered Surveyors
* Chartered Institute of Arbitrators

* Delete all but one

(If no appointor is selected the appointor shall be the President or a Vice-President of the Royal Institute of British Architects.)

Article 7B

Dispute or difference – legal proceedings

[h] Subject to article 6, if any dispute or difference as to any matter or thing of whatsoever nature arising under this Agreement or in connection therewith shall arise between the parties either during the progress or after the completion or abandonment of the Works or after the determination of the employment of the Contractor it shall be determined by legal proceedings.

---

[h] If disputes are to be decided by arbitration delete article 7B. If disputes are to be decided by legal proceedings delete article 7A.

Article 7C

Dispute or difference – fallback position

If neither Article 7A nor Article 7B is deleted by the parties then Article 7A (arbitration) will apply.

Notes	
	[A1] AS WITNESS THE HANDS OF THE PARTIES HERETO
[A1] For Agreement executed under hand and NOT as a deed.	[A1] Signed by or on behalf of the Employer_____ in the presence of: [A1] Signed by or on behalf of the Contractor_____ in the presence of:

[A2] For Agreement executed as a deed under the law of England and Wales by a company or other body corporate: insert the name of the party mentioned and identified on page 1 and then use *either* [A3] and [A4] *or* [A5]. If the party is an *individual* see note [A6].	**[A2] EXECUTED AS A DEED BY THE EMPLOYER** [A6] hereinbefore mentioned namely_____ [A3] by affixing hereto its common seal [A4] in the presence of:
[A3] For use if the party is using its common seal, which should be affixed under the party's name.	
[A4] For use of the party's officers authorised to affix its common seal.	* OR —
[A5] For use if the party is a company registered under the Companies Acts which is not using a common seal: insert the names of the two officers by whom the company is acting *who MUST be either a director and the company secretary or two directors*, and insert their signatures with 'Director' or 'Secretary' as appropriate. *This method of execution is NOT valid for local authorities or certain other bodies incorporated by Act of Parliament or by charter if exempted under s.718(2) of the Companies Act 1985.*	[A5] acting by a director and its secretary* / two directors* whose signatures are here subscribed: namely _____ [Signature] _____ DIRECTOR and _____ [Signature] _____ SECRETARY* / DIRECTOR* **[A2] AND AS A DEED BY THE CONTRACTOR** [A6] hereinbefore mentioned namely _____ [A3] by affixing hereto its common seal [A4] in the presence of:
[A6] If executed as a deed by an *individual*: insert the name at [A2], delete the words at [A3], substitute 'whose signature is here subscribed' and insert the individual's signature. The individual MUST sign in the presence of a witness who attests the signature. Insert at [A4] the signature and name of the witness. Sealing by an individual is not required.	* OR — [A5] acting by a director and its secretary* / two directors* whose signatures are here subscribed: namely _____ [Signature] _____ DIRECTOR and _____ [Signature] _____ SECRETARY* / DIRECTOR* * *Delete as appropriate*

Conditions hereinbefore referred to

1 Intentions of the parties

Contractor's obligations

1·1 ·1 The Contractor shall with due diligence and in a good and workmanlike manner and, where alternative A in the 5th recital applies, in accordance with the Health and Safety Plan of the Principal Contractor carry out and complete the Works in accordance with the Contract Documents using materials and workmanship of the quality and standards therein specified provided that where and to the extent that approval of the quality of materials or of the standards of workmanship is a matter for the opinion of the Architect/the Contract Administrator such quality and standards shall be to the reasonable satisfaction of the Architect/the Contract Administrator.

1·1 ·2 The Contractor shall take all reasonable steps to encourage employees and agents of the Contractor and sub-contractors employed in the execution of the Works to be registered cardholders under the Construction Skills Certification Scheme (CSCS) or any successor, or qualified under an equivalent recognised qualification scheme.

Architect's/Contract Administrator's duties

1·2 The Architect/The Contract Administrator shall issue any further information necessary for the proper carrying out of the Works, issue all certificates and confirm all instructions in writing in accordance with these Conditions.

Reappointment of Planning Supervisor or Principal Contractor – notification to Contractor

1·3 If the Employer pursuant to article 4 or article 5 by a further appointment replaces the Planning Supervisor referred to in, or appointed pursuant to, article 4 or replaces the Contractor or any other contractor appointed as the Principal Contractor, the Employer shall immediately upon such further appointment notify the Contractor in writing of the name and address of the new appointee.

Alternative B in the 5th recital – notification by Contractor – regulation 7(5) of the CDM Regulations

1·4 Where Alternative B in the 5th recital applies the Contractor shall, if applicable, give the notice to the Health and Safety Executive required by regulation 7(5) of the CDM Regulations and such notice shall be in accordance with regulations 7(6)(a) and (b) of the CDM Regulations. The notice shall be given (with a copy to the Employer and to the Architect/ the Contract Administrator) before the Contractor or any person under his control starts to carry out any construction work.

Giving or service of notices or other documents

1·5 Where this Agreement does not specifically state the manner of giving or service of any notice or other document required or authorised in pursuance of this Agreement such notice or other document shall be given or served by any effective means to any agreed address. If no address has been agreed then if given or served by being addressed pre-paid and delivered by post to the addressee's last known principal business address or, where the addressee is a body corporate, to the body's registered or principal office it shall be treated as having been effectively given or served.

Reckoning periods of days

1·6 ·1 Where under this Agreement an act is required to be done within a specified period of days after or from a specified date, the period shall begin immediately after that date. Where the period would include a day which is a Public Holiday that day shall be excluded.

·2 A 'Public Holiday' shall mean Christmas Day, Good Friday or a day which under the Banking and Financial Dealings Act 1971 is a bank holiday. [i]

Applicable law

1·7 Whatever the nationality, residence or domicile of the Employer, the Contractor or any sub-contractor or supplier and wherever the Works are situated the law of England shall be the law applicable to this Agreement. [j]

Contracts (Rights of Third Parties) Act 1999 – contracting out

1·8 Notwithstanding any other provision of this Agreement nothing in this Agreement confers or purports to confer any right to enforce any of its terms on any person who is not a party to it.

2 Commencement and completion

Commencement and completion

2·1 The Works may be commenced on

....

and shall be completed by

....

Extension of contract period

2·2 If it becomes apparent that the Works will not be completed by the date for completion inserted in clause 2·1 hereof (or any later date fixed in accordance with the provisions of this clause 2·2) for reasons beyond the control of the Contractor, including compliance with any instruction of the Architect/the Contract Administrator under this Agreement whose issue is not due to a default of the Contractor, then the Contractor shall thereupon in writing so notify the Architect/the Contract

---

[i] Amend as necessary if different Public Holidays are applicable.

[j] Where the parties do not wish the law applicable to this Agreement to be the law of England appropriate amendments to clause 1·7 should be made.

2·2 *continued*

Administrator who shall make, in writing, such extension of time for completion as may be reasonable. Reasons within the control of the Contractor include any default of the Contractor or of others employed or engaged by or under him for or in connection with the Works and of any supplier of goods or materials for the Works.

Damages for non-completion

2·3 If the Works are not completed by the completion date inserted in clause 2·1 hereof or by any later completion date fixed under clause 2·2 hereof the Contractor shall pay or allow to the Employer liquidated damages at the rate of

£ .... per ....[k] between the aforesaid completion date and the date of practical completion.

The Employer may

either

recover the liquidated damages from the Contractor as a debt

or

deduct the liquidated damages from any monies due to the Contractor under this Agreement provided that a notice of deduction pursuant to clause 4·4·2 or clause 4·5·1·3 has been given. If the Employer intends to deduct any such damages from the sum stated as due in the final certificate, he shall additionally inform the Contractor, in writing, of that intention not later than the date of issue of the final certificate.

Practical completion

2·4 The Architect/The Contract Administrator shall certify the date when in his opinion the Works have reached practical completion and the Contractor has complied sufficiently with clause 5·9.

Defects liability

2·5 Any defects, excessive shrinkages or other faults to the Works which appear within 3 months/

....[l] of the date of practical completion and are due to materials or workmanship not in accordance with this Agreement or frost occurring before practical completion shall be notified by the Architect/the Contract Administrator to the Contractor who shall make good entirely at his own cost unless the Architect/the Contract Administrator shall otherwise instruct.

The Architect/The Contract Administrator shall certify the date when in his opinion the Contractor's obligations under this clause 2·5 have been discharged.

---

[k] Insert 'day', 'week' or other period.

[l] If a different period is required delete '3 months' and insert the appropriate period.

3 Control of the Works

Assignment

3·1 Neither the Employer nor the Contractor shall, without the written consent of the other, assign this Agreement.

Sub-contracting

3·2 ·1 The Contractor shall not sub-contract the Works or any part thereof without the written consent of the Architect/the Contract Administrator whose consent shall not be unreasonably delayed or withheld.

·2 A sub-contract for the Works or any part thereof shall provide that if the Contractor fails properly to pay the amount, or any part thereof, due to the sub-contractor by the final date for its payment stated in the sub-contract, the Contractor shall pay to the sub-contractor in addition to the amount not properly paid simple interest thereon for the period until such payment is made; that the payment of such simple interest shall be treated as a debt due to the sub-contractor by the Contractor; that the rate of interest payable shall be five per cent (5%) over the Base Rate of the Bank of England which is current at the date the payment by the Contractor became overdue; and that any payment of simple interest shall not in any circumstances be construed as a waiver by the sub-contractor of his right to proper payment of the principal amount due from the Contractor to the sub-contractor in accordance with, and within the time stated in, the sub-contract or of any rights of the sub-contractor under the sub-contract in regard to suspension of the performance of his obligations to the Contractor under the sub-contract or determination of his employment for the failure by the Contractor properly to pay any amount due under the sub-contract to the sub-contractor.

Contractor's representative

3·3 The Contractor shall at all reasonable times keep upon the Works a competent person in charge and any instructions given to him by the Architect/the Contract Administrator shall be deemed to have been issued to the Contractor.

Exclusion from the Works

3·4 The Architect/The Contract Administrator may (but not unreasonably or vexatiously) issue instructions requiring the exclusion from the Works of any person employed thereon.

Architect's/Contract Administrator's instructions

3·5 The Architect/The Contract Administrator may issue written instructions which the Contractor shall forthwith carry out. If instructions are given orally they shall, within 2 days, be confirmed in writing by the Architect/the Contract Administrator.

If within 7 days after receipt of a written notice from the Architect/the Contract Administrator requiring compliance with an instruction the Contractor does not comply therewith then the Employer may employ and pay other persons to carry out the work and all costs incurred thereby may be deducted by

3·5 *continued*

him from any monies due or to become due to the Contractor under this Agreement or shall be recoverable from the Contractor by the Employer as a debt.

Correction of inconsistencies

3·6 Any inconsistency in or between the Contract Drawings [m] and the Contract Specification [m] and the schedules [m] shall be corrected and any such correction which results in an addition, omission or other change shall be treated as a variation under clause 3·7 hereof. Nothing contained in the Contract Drawings [m] or the Contract Specification [m] or the schedules [m] shall override, modify or affect in any way whatsoever the application or interpretation of that which is contained in these Conditions.

Variations

3·7 The Architect/The Contract Administrator may, without invalidating this Agreement, order an addition to or omission from or other change in the Works or the order or period in which they are to be carried out and any such instruction shall be valued by the Architect/the Contract Administrator on a fair and reasonable basis, using where relevant prices in the priced Specification/schedules/schedule of rates [m], and such valuation shall include any direct loss and/or expense incurred by the Contractor due to the regular progress of the Works being affected by compliance with such instruction or due to the compliance or non-compliance by the Employer with clause 5·6.

Instead of the valuation referred to above, the price may be agreed between the Architect/the Contract Administrator and the Contractor prior to the Contractor carrying out any such instruction.

Provisional sums

3·8 The Architect/The Contract Administrator shall issue instructions as to the expenditure of any provisional sums and such instructions shall be valued or the price agreed in accordance with clause 3·7 hereof.

4 Payment

Payments subject to Supplemental Condition C

4·1 Where at the date of this Agreement the Employer is a 'contractor' for the purposes of the Construction Industry Scheme (CIS) or if at any time up to the payment of the final certificate the Employer becomes such a 'contractor' the obligation of the Employer to make any payments under or pursuant to this Agreement is subject to Supplemental Condition C.

Progress payments and retention

4·2 ·1 The Architect/The Contract Administrator shall, at intervals of 4 weeks calculated from the date for commencement, certify progress payments of 95%/...............%[o] of the total value of the work properly executed, including any amounts either ascertained or agreed under clauses 3·7 and 3·8 hereof, and the value of any materials and goods which have been reasonably and properly brought upon

4·2 ·1 *continued*

the site for the purpose of the Works and which are adequately stored and protected against the weather and other casualties, less the total amounts due to the Contractor in certificates of progress payment previously issued. The certificate shall state to what the progress payment relates and the basis on which the amount of the progress payment was calculated. The final date for payment by the Employer of the amount so certified shall be 14 days from the date of issue of the certificate. The provisions of clause 4·4 shall apply to any certificate issued pursuant to this clause 4·2·1.

·2 If the Employer fails properly to pay the amount, or any part thereof, due to the Contractor under this Agreement by the final date for its payment the Employer shall pay to the Contractor in addition to the amount not properly paid simple interest thereon for the period until such payment is made. Payment of such simple interest shall be treated as a debt due to the Contractor by the Employer. The rate of interest payable shall be five per cent (5%) over the Base Rate of the Bank of England which is current at the date the payment by the Employer became overdue. Any payment of simple interest under this clause 4·2·2 shall not in any circumstances be construed as a waiver by the Contractor of his right to proper payment of the principal amount due from the Employer to the Contractor in accordance with, and within the time stated in, the Conditions or of the rights of the Contractor in regard to suspension of performance of his obligations under this Agreement to the Employer pursuant to clause 4·8 or to determination of his employment pursuant to the default referred to in clause 7·3·1·1.

Penultimate certificate

4·3 The Architect/The Contract Administrator shall within 14 days after the date of practical completion certified under clause 2·4 hereof certify payment as an amount due to the Contractor of 97½%/...............% [o] of the total amount to be paid to the Contractor under this Agreement so far as that amount is ascertainable at the date of practical completion including any amounts either ascertained or agreed under clauses 3·7 and 3·8 hereof less the total amounts due to the Contractor in certificates of progress payment previously issued. The penultimate certificate shall state to what the progress payment relates and the basis on which the amount of the certificate was calculated. The final date for payment by the Employer of the amount so certified shall be 14 days from the date of issue of that certificate. If the Employer fails properly to pay the amount, or any

---

[m] Delete as appropriate to follow any deletions in the recitals on page 3.

[n] Not used.

[o] The alternative should be completed where a percentage other than 95% applies in clause 4·2·1.

4·3 *continued*

part thereof, due to the Contractor by the final date for its payment the provisions of clause 4·2·2 shall apply. The provisions of clause 4·4 shall apply to the certificate issued pursuant to this clause 4·3.

Notices of amounts to be paid and deductions

4·4 ·1 Not later than 5 days after the issue of a certificate of payment pursuant to clauses 4·2·1 and 4·3 the Employer shall give a written notice to the Contractor which shall specify the amount of the payment proposed to be made in respect of the amount stated as due in that certificate.

·2 Not later than 5 days before the final date for payment of the amount due pursuant to clause 4·2 or clause 4·3 the Employer may give a written notice to the Contractor which shall specify any amount proposed to be withheld and/or deducted from that notified amount, the ground or grounds for such withholding and/or deduction and the amount of the withholding and/or deduction attributable to each ground.

·3 Where the Employer does not give a written notice pursuant to clause 4·4·1 and/or to clause 4·4·2 the Employer shall pay the amount stated as due in the certificate.

Final certificate

4·5 ·1 ·1 The Contractor shall supply within 3 months/...[p] from the date of practical completion all documentation reasonably required for the computation of the amount to be finally certified by the Architect/the Contract Administrator and the Architect/the Contract Administrator shall within 28 days of receipt of such documentation, provided that the Architect/the Contract Administrator has issued the certificate under clause 2·5 hereof, issue a final certificate certifying the amount remaining due to the Contractor or due to the Employer as the case may be and shall state to what the amount relates and the basis on which that amount was calculated.

·2 Not later than 5 days after the date of issue of the final certificate the Employer shall give a written notice to the Contractor which shall specify the amount of the payment proposed to be made to the Contractor in respect of the amount certified.

·3 The final date for payment of such amount as a debt payable as the case may be by the Employer to the Contractor or by the Contractor to the Employer shall be 14 days from the date of issue of the said certificate. Not later than 5 days before the final date for payment of the amount due to the Contractor the Employer may give a written notice to the Contractor which shall specify any

4·5 ·1 ·3 *continued*

amount proposed to be withheld and/or deducted therefrom, the ground or grounds for such withholding and/or deduction and the amount of the withholding and/or deduction attributable to each ground.

·4 Where the Employer does not give a written notice pursuant to clause 4·5·1·2 and/or to clause 4·5·1·3 the Employer shall pay the Contractor the amount stated as due to the Contractor in the final certificate.

·2 If the Employer or the Contractor fails properly to pay the debt, or any part thereof, by the final date for its payment the Employer or the Contractor as the case may be shall pay to the other in addition to the debt not properly paid simple interest thereon for the period until such payment is made. The rate of interest payable shall be five per cent (5%) over the Base Rate of the Bank of England which is current at the date the payment by the Employer or by the Contractor as the case may be became overdue. Any payment of simple interest under this clause 4·5·2 shall not in any circumstances be construed as a waiver by the Contractor or by the Employer as the case may be of his right to proper payment of the aforesaid debt due from the Employer to the Contractor or from the Contractor to the Employer in accordance with clause 4·5·1.

Contribution, levy and tax changes [q]

4·6 Contribution, levy and tax changes shall be dealt with by the application of Supplemental Condition A. The percentage addition under clause A5 is...............%.

Fixed price

4·7 No account shall be taken in any payment to the Contractor under this Agreement of any change in the cost to the Contractor of the labour, materials, plant and other resources employed in carrying out the Works except as provided in clause 4·6, if applicable.

Right of suspension by Contractor

4·8 If, subject to any notice issued pursuant to clause 4·4·2, the Employer shall fail to pay the amount due certified under either clause 4·2·1 or clause 4·3 in full by the final date for payment as required by this Agreement and such failure shall continue for 7 days after the Contractor has given to the Employer, with a copy to the Architect/the Contractor Administrator, written notice of his intention to suspend performance of his obligations under this Agreement to the Employer and the ground or grounds on which it is intended

---

[p] If a different period is required delete '3 months' and insert the appropriate period.

[q] Delete clause 4·6 if the contract period is of such limited duration as to make the provisions of Supplemental Condition A inapplicable.

4·8 *continued*

to suspend performance, then the Contractor may suspend such performance of his obligations under this Agreement until payment in full occurs.

5 Statutory obligations

Statutory obligations, notices, fees and charges

5·1 The Contractor shall comply with, and give all notices required by, any statute, any statutory instrument, rule or order or any regulation or byelaw applicable to the Works (hereinafter called the 'statutory requirements') and shall pay all fees and charges in respect of the Works legally recoverable from him.

If the Contractor finds any divergence between the statutory requirements and the Contract Documents or between the statutory requirements and any instruction of the Architect/the Contract Administrator he shall immediately give to the Architect/the Contract Administrator a written notice specifying the divergence.

Subject to this latter obligation, the Contractor shall not be liable to the Employer under this Agreement if the Works do not comply with the statutory requirements where and to the extent that such non-compliance of the Works results from the Contractor having carried out work in accordance with the Contract Documents or any instruction of the Architect/the Contract Administrator.

Value added tax

5·2 The sum or sums due to the Contractor under article 2 of this Agreement shall be exclusive of any value added tax and the Employer shall pay to the Contractor any value added tax properly chargeable by the Commissioners of Customs and Excise on the supply to the Employer of any goods and services by the Contractor under this Agreement in the manner set out in Supplemental Condition B. Clause B1·1 applies/does not apply [r].

Construction Industry Scheme (CIS)

5·3 Supplemental Condition C shall apply where at the date of this Agreement the Employer is a 'contractor' or if at any time before the payment of the final certificate the Employer becomes a 'contractor' for the purposes of the Construction Industry Scheme (CIS) referred to in Supplemental Condition C.

5·4 [Number not used]

Prevention of corruption

5·5 The Employer shall be entitled to cancel this Agreement and to recover from the Contractor the amount of any loss resulting from such cancellation if the Contractor shall have offered or given or agreed to give to any person any gift or consideration of any kind or if the Contractor shall have committed any offence under the Prevention of Corruption Acts 1889 to 1916 or, if the Employer is a local authority, shall have given any fee or reward the receipt of which is an offence under sub-section (2) of section 117 of the Local Government Act 1972 or any re-enactment thereof.

Provisions for use where Alternative A in the 5th recital applies

Employer's obligation – Planning Supervisor – Principal Contractor

5·6 The Employer shall ensure:

that the Planning Supervisor carries out all the duties of a planning supervisor under the CDM Regulations; and

where the Contractor is not the Principal Contractor, that the Principal Contractor carries out all the duties of a principal contractor under the CDM Regulations.

Duty of Principal Contractor

5·7 Where the Contractor is and while he remains the Principal Contractor, the Contractor shall comply with all the duties of a principal contractor set out in the CDM Regulations. Without prejudice to this obligation the Principal Contractor shall ensure that the health and safety plan of the Planning Supervisor provided to him is developed by him to comply with regulation 15(4) of the CDM Regulations (the 'Health and Safety Plan') and is supplied to the Employer before the Contractor or any person under his control starts to carry out any construction work; and that this Health and Safety Plan continues during the progress of the Works to have the features required by regulation 15(4) of the CDM Regulations. Any amendment by the Principal Contractor to the Health and Safety Plan shall be notified to the Employer who shall where relevant thereupon notify the Planning Supervisor and the Architect/the Contract Administrator.

Successor appointed to the Contractor as the Principal Contractor

5·8 Clause 5·8 applies from the time the Employer pursuant to article 5 appoints a successor to the Contractor as the Principal Contractor. The Contractor shall comply at no cost to the Employer with all the reasonable requirements of the Principal Contractor to the extent that such requirements are necessary for compliance with the CDM Regulations; and, notwithstanding clause 2·2, no extension of time shall be given in respect of such compliance.

Health and safety file

5·9 Within the time reasonably required in writing by the Planning Supervisor to the Contractor, the Contractor shall provide, and shall ensure that any sub-contractor, through the Contractor, provides, such information to the Planning Supervisor or, if the Contractor is not the Principal Contractor, to the Principal Contractor as the Planning Supervisor reasonably requires for the preparation, pursuant to regulations 14(d), 14(e) and 14(f) of the CDM Regulations, of the health and safety file required by the CDM Regulations.

---

[r] Delete as required. Clause B1·1 can only apply where the Contractor is satisfied at the date this Agreement is entered into that his output tax on all supplies to the Employer under this Agreement will be at either a positive or a zero rate of tax.

6 Injury, damage and insurance

Injury to or death of persons

6·1 The Contractor shall be liable for, and shall indemnify the Employer against, any expense, liability, loss, claim or proceedings whatsoever arising under any statute or at common law in respect of personal injury to or death of any person whomsoever arising out of or in the course of or caused by the carrying out of the Works, except to the extent that the same is due to any act or neglect of the Employer or of any person for whom the Employer is responsible.

Without prejudice to his liability to indemnify the Employer the Contractor shall take out and maintain and shall cause any sub-contractor to take out and maintain insurance which in respect of claims for personal injury to or the death of any person under a contract of service or apprenticeship with the Contractor, and arising out of and in the course of such person's employment, shall comply with all relevant legislation and, in respect of any other liability for personal injury or death, shall be such as is necessary to cover the liability of the Contractor or, as the case may be, of such sub-contractor.

Injury or damage to property

6·2 The Contractor shall be liable for, and shall indemnify the Employer against, any expense, liability, loss, claim or proceedings in respect of any loss, injury or damage whatsoever to any property real or personal (other than loss, injury or damage to the Works or to any unfixed materials and goods delivered to, placed on or adjacent to the Works and intended therefor or, where clause 6·3B is applicable, to any property required to be insured pursuant to clause 6·3B for the perils therein listed) in so far as such loss, injury or damage arises out of or in the course of or by reason of the carrying out of the Works and to the extent that the same is due to any negligence, breach of statutory duty, omission or default of the Contractor, his servants or agents, or of any person employed or engaged by the Contractor upon or in connection with the Works or any part thereof, his servants or agents.

Without prejudice to his obligation to indemnify the Employer, the Contractor shall take out and maintain and shall cause any sub-contractor to take out and maintain insurance in respect of the liability referred to above in respect of loss, injury or damage to any property real or personal other than the Works (or where clause 6·3B is applicable other than any property required to be insured pursuant to clause 6·3B for the perils therein listed). The insurance cover to which clause 6·2 applies:

- shall indemnify the Employer in like manner to the Contractor but only to the extent that the Contractor may be liable to indemnify the Employer under the terms of this Agreement; and

- shall, for any one occurrence or series of occurrences arising out of one event, be not less than:

    £ ....

Insurance of the Works by Contractor – Fire etc. [s] [t]

6·3A The Contractor shall in the joint names of Employer and Contractor insure the Works and all unfixed materials and goods delivered to, placed on or adjacent to the Works and intended therefor against loss and damage by fire, lightning, explosion, storm, tempest, flood, bursting or overflowing of water tanks, apparatus or pipes, earthquake, aircraft and other aerial devices or articles dropped therefrom, riot and civil commotion, for the full reinstatement value thereof plus ....% [u] to cover professional fees.

After any inspection required by the insurers in respect of a claim under the insurance mentioned in this clause 6·3A the Contractor shall with due diligence restore or replace work or materials or goods damaged and dispose of any debris and proceed with and complete the Works. The Contractor shall not be entitled to any payment in respect of work or materials or goods damaged or the disposal of any debris other than the monies received under the said insurance (less only the amount properly incurred by the Employer in respect of professional fees but not exceeding the amount arrived at by applying the percentage to cover professional fees stated in clause 6·3A to the amount of the monies so paid excluding any amount included therein for professional fees) and such monies shall be paid to the Contractor under certificates of the Architect/the Contract Administrator at the periods stated in clause 4.

Insurance of the Works and any existing structures by Employer – Fire etc. [s]

6·3B The Employer shall in the joint names of Employer and Contractor insure against loss or damage to any existing structures (together with any contents owned by him or for which he is responsible) and to the Works and all unfixed materials and goods delivered to, placed on or adjacent to the Works and intended therefor by fire, lightning, explosion, storm, tempest, flood, bursting or overflowing of water tanks, apparatus or pipes, earthquake, aircraft and other aerial devices or articles dropped therefrom, riot and civil commotion.

---

[s] **Delete** clause 6·3A

where the Works are an extension to or an alteration of an existing structure and the Employer can obtain the insurance in compliance with the requirement in clause 6·3B.

Delete clause 6·3B

where the Works are not an extension to or an alteration of an existing structure

or

where the Employer cannot obtain the insurance in compliance with the requirement in clause 6·3B.

[t] Where the Contractor has in force an All Risks Policy which insures the Works against loss or damage by *inter alia* the perils referred to in clause 6·3A, this Policy may be used to provide the insurance required by clause 6·3A provided the Policy recognises the Employer as a joint insured with the Contractor in respect of the Works and the Policy is maintained.

[u] Percentage to be inserted.

6·3B *continued*

If any loss or damage as referred to in this clause 6·3B occurs to the Works or to any unfixed materials and goods delivered to, placed on or adjacent to the Works and intended therefor then the Architect/the Contract Administrator shall issue instructions for the reinstatement and making good of such loss or damage in accordance with clause 3·5 hereof and such instructions shall be valued under clause 3·7 hereof.

Evidence of insurance

6·4 The Contractor shall produce, and shall cause any sub-contractor to produce, such evidence as the Employer may reasonably require that the insurances referred to in clauses 6·1 and 6·2 and, where applicable, 6·3A hereof have been taken out and are in force at all material times. Where clause 6·3B hereof is applicable the Employer shall produce such evidence as the Contractor may reasonably require that the insurance referred to therein has been taken out and is in force at all material times.

7 Determination

Notices

7·1 Any notice or further notice to which clauses 7·2·1, 7·2·2, 7·3·1 and 7·3·2 refer shall be in writing and given by actual delivery, or by special delivery or by recorded delivery. If sent by special delivery or recorded delivery the notice or further notice shall, subject to proof to the contrary, be deemed to have been received 48 hours after the date of posting (excluding Saturday and Sunday and Public Holidays).

Determination by Employer

7·2 ·1 If the Contractor without reasonable cause makes default by failing to proceed diligently with the Works or by wholly or substantially suspending the carrying out of the Works before practical completion or by failing, pursuant to the Conditions, to comply with the requirements of the CDM Regulations, the Architect/the Contract Administrator may give notice to the Contractor which specifies the default and requires it to be ended. If the default is not ended within 7 days of receipt of the notice the Employer may by further notice to the Contractor determine the employment of the Contractor under this Agreement. Such determination shall take effect on the date of receipt of the further notice. A notice of determination under clause 7·2·1 shall not be given unreasonably or vexatiously.

·2 If the Contractor

makes a composition or arrangement with his creditors, or becomes bankrupt, or,

being a company,

makes a proposal for a voluntary arrangement for a composition of debts or scheme of arrangement to be approved in accordance with the Companies Act 1985 or the

7·2 ·2 *continued*

Insolvency Act 1986 as the case may be or any amendment or re-enactment thereof, or

has a provisional liquidator appointed, or

has a winding-up order made, or

passes a resolution for voluntary winding-up (except for the purposes of amalgamation or reconstruction), or

under the Insolvency Act 1986 or any amendment or re-enactment thereof has an administrator or an administrative receiver appointed

the Employer may by notice to the Contractor determine the employment of the Contractor under this Agreement. Such determination shall take effect on the date of receipt of such notice.

·3 Upon determination of the employment of the Contractor under clause 7·2·1 or clause 7·2·2 the Contractor shall immediately cease to occupy the site of the Works and the Employer shall not be bound to make any further payment to the Contractor that may be due under this Agreement until after completion of the Works and the making good of any defects therein. The Employer may recover from the Contractor the additional cost to him of completing the Works and any expenses properly incurred by the Employer as a result of, and any direct loss and/or damage caused to the Employer by, the determination.

·4 The provisions of clauses 7·2·1 to 7·2·3 are without prejudice to any other rights and remedies which the Employer may possess.

Determination by Contractor

7·3 ·1 If the Employer makes default in any one or more of the following respects:

·1 he does not pay by the final date for payment the amount properly due to the Contractor in respect of any certificate or pay any VAT due on that amount pursuant to clause 5·2 and Supplemental Condition B;

·2 he, or any person for whom he is responsible, interferes with or obstructs the issue of any certificate due under this Agreement or interferes with or obstructs the carrying out of the Works or fails to make the premises available for the Contractor in accordance with clause 2·1 hereof;

·3 he suspends the carrying out of the whole or substantially the whole of the Works for a continuous period of one month or more;

·4 he fails, pursuant to the Conditions, to comply with the requirements of the CDM Regulations,

7·3 ·1 *continued*

the Contractor may give notice to the Employer which specifies the default and requires it to be ended. If the default is not ended within 7 days of receipt of the notice the Contractor may by further notice to the Employer determine the employment of the Contractor under this Agreement. Such determination shall take effect on the date of receipt of the further notice. A notice of determination under clause 7·3·1 shall not be given unreasonably or vexatiously.

·2 If the Employer

makes a composition or arrangement with his creditors, or becomes bankrupt, or,

being a company,

makes a proposal for a voluntary arrangement for a composition of debts or scheme of arrangement to be approved in accordance with the Companies Act 1985 or the Insolvency Act 1986 as the case may be or any amendment or re-enactment thereof, or

has a provisional liquidator appointed, or

has a winding-up order made, or

passes a resolution for voluntary winding-up (except for the purposes of amalgamation or reconstruction), or

under the Insolvency Act 1986 or any amendment or re-enactment thereof has an administrator or an administrative receiver appointed

the Contractor may by notice to the Employer determine the employment of the Contractor under this Agreement. Such determination shall take effect on the date of receipt of such notice.

·3 Upon determination of the employment of the Contractor under clause 7·3·1 or clause 7·3·2 the Contractor shall prepare an account setting out:

– the total value of work properly executed and of materials and goods properly brought on the site for the purpose of the Works, such value to be ascertained in accordance with this Agreement as if the employment of the Contractor had not been determined, together with any amounts due to the Contractor under the Conditions not included in such total value; and

– the cost to the Contractor of removing or having removed from the site all temporary buildings, plant, tools and equipment; and

– any direct loss and/or damage caused to the Contractor by the determination.

7·3 ·3 *continued*

After taking into account amounts previously paid to the Contractor under this Agreement, the Employer shall pay to the Contractor the full amount properly due in respect of this account within 28 days of its submission by the Contractor.

·4 The provisions of clauses 7·3·1 to 7·3·3 are without prejudice to any other rights and remedies which the Contractor may possess.

8 Settlement of disputes [v]

Adjudication

8·1 Pursuant to article 6 the procedures for adjudication are set out in Supplemental Condition D.

Arbitration

8·2 Pursuant to article 7A the procedures for arbitration are set out in Supplemental Condition E.

Legal proceedings

8·3 Where article 7B applies, any dispute or difference shall be determined by legal proceedings pursuant to article 7B.

---

[v] It is open to the Employer and the Contractor to resolve disputes by the process of Mediation: see Practice Note 28 'Mediation on a Building Contract or Sub-Contract Dispute'.

Supplemental Conditions

A: CONTRIBUTION, LEVY AND TAX CHANGES
Clause 4·6

Deemed calculation of Contract Sum – rates of contribution etc.

A1 The sum referred to in article 2 (in this Supplemental Condition A called the 'Contract Sum') shall be deemed to have been calculated in the manner set out below and shall be subject to adjustment in the events specified hereunder:

A1·1 The prices used or set out by the Contractor in the Contract Documents are based upon the types and rates of contribution, levy and tax payable by a person in his capacity as an employer and which at the date of this Agreement are payable by the Contractor. A type and rate so payable are in clause A1·2 referred to as a 'tender type' and a 'tender rate'.

Increases or decreases in rates of contribution etc. – payment or allowance

A1·2 If any of the tender rates, other than a rate of levy payable by virtue of the Industrial Training Act 1964, is increased or decreased, or if a tender type ceases to be payable, or if a new type of contribution, levy or tax which is payable by a person in his capacity as an employer becomes payable after the date of tender, [w] then in any such case the net amount of the difference between what the Contractor actually pays or will pay in respect of

·1 workpeople [w] engaged upon or in connection with the Works either on or adjacent to the site of the Works and

·2 workpeople [w] directly employed by the Contractor who are engaged upon the production of materials or goods [w] for use in or in connection with the Works and who operate neither on nor adjacent to the site of the Works and to the extent that they are so engaged

or because of his employment of such workpeople and what he would have paid had the alteration, cessation or new type of contribution, levy or tax not become effective shall, as the case may be, be paid to or allowed by the Contractor.

Persons employed on site other than 'workpeople'

A1·3 There shall be added to the net amount paid to or allowed by the Contractor under clause A1·2 in respect of each person employed on the site by the Contractor for the Works and who is not within the definition of 'workpeople' in clause A4·6·3 the same amount as is payable or allowable in respect of a craftsman under clause A1·2 or such proportion of that amount as reflects the time (measured in whole working days) that each such person is so employed.

A1·4 For the purposes of clause A1·3

no period less than 2 whole working days in any week shall be taken into account and periods less than a whole working day shall not be aggregated to amount to a whole working day;

the phrase "the same amount as is payable or allowable in respect of a craftsman" shall refer to the amount in respect of a craftsman employed by the Contractor (or by any sub-contractor under a sub-contract to which clause A3 refers) under the rules or decisions or agreements of the Construction Industry Joint Council or other wage-fixing body [w] and, where the aforesaid rules or decisions or agreements provide for more than one rate of wage emolument or other expense for a craftsman, shall refer to the amount in respect of a craftsman employed as aforesaid to whom the highest rate is applicable; and

the phrase "employed . . . by the Contractor" shall mean an employment to which the Income Tax (Employment) Regulations 1993 (the PAYE Regulations) under section 203 of the Income and Corporation Taxes Act 1988 apply.

Refunds and premiums

A1·5 The prices used or set out by the Contractor in the Contract Documents are based upon the types and rates of refund of the contributions, levies and taxes payable by a person in his capacity as an employer and upon the types and rates of premium receivable by a person in his capacity as an employer being in each case types and rates which at the date of tender are receivable by the Contractor. Such a type and such a rate are in clause A1·6 referred to as a 'tender type' and a 'tender rate'.

A1·6 If any of the tender rates is increased or decreased or if a tender type ceases to be payable or if a new type of refund of any contribution, levy or tax payable by a person in his capacity as an employer becomes receivable or if a new type of premium receivable by a person in his capacity as an employer becomes receivable after the date of tender, then in any such case the net amount of the difference between what the Contractor actually receives or will receive in respect of workpeople as referred to in clauses A1·2·1 and A1·2·2 or because of his employment of such workpeople and what he would have received had the alteration, cessation or new type of refund or premium not become effective shall, as the case may be, be allowed by or paid to the Contractor.

A1·7 The references in clauses A1·5 and A1·6 to premiums shall be construed as meaning all payments howsoever they are described which are made under or by virtue of an Act of Parliament to a person in his capacity as an employer and which affect the cost to an employer of having persons in his employment.

Contracted-out employment

A1·8 Where employer's contributions are payable by the Contractor in respect of workpeople as referred to in clauses A1·2·1 and A1·2·2 whose employment is contracted-out employment within the meaning of the Social Security Pensions Act 1975 the Contractor shall for the purpose of recovery or allowance under this clause be deemed to pay employer's contributions as if that employment were not contracted-out employment.

Meaning of contribution etc.

A1·9 The references in clause A1 to contribution, levies and taxes shall be construed as meaning all impositions payable by a person in his capacity as an employer howsoever they are described and whoever the recipient which are imposed under or by virtue of an Act of Parliament and which affect the cost to an employer of having persons in his employment.

---

[w] See clause A4·6.

Materials – duties and taxes

A2·1 The contract sum is based upon the types and rates of duty, if any, and tax, if any (other than any value added tax which is treated, or is capable of being treated, as input tax by the Contractor), by whomsoever payable which at the date of tender are payable on the import, purchase, sale, appropriation, processing, use or disposal of the materials, goods, electricity, fuels, materials taken from the site as waste or any other solid, liquid or gas necessary for the execution of the Works by virtue of any Act of Parliament. A type and a rate so payable are in clause A2·2 referred to as a 'tender type' and a 'tender rate'.

A2·2 If, in relation to any materials or goods [w] or any electricity or fuels or materials taken from the site as waste or any other solid, liquid or gas necessary for the execution of the Works including temporary site installations for those Works, a tender rate is increased or decreased or a tender type ceases to be payable or a new type of duty or tax (other than any valued added tax which is treated, or is capable of being treated, as input tax by the Contractor) becomes payable on the import, purchase, sale, appropriation, processing, use or disposal of any of the above things after the date of tender, then in any such case the net amount of the difference between what the Contractor actually pays in respect of those materials, goods, electricity, fuels, materials taken from the site as waste or any other solid, liquid or gas and what he would have paid in respect of them had the alteration, cessation or imposition not occurred shall, as the case may be, be paid to or allowed by the Contractor. In this clause A2·2 the expression "a new type of duty or tax" includes an additional duty or tax and a duty or tax imposed in regard to any of the above in respect of which no duty or tax whatever was previously payable (other than any value added tax which is treated, or is capable of being treated, as input tax by the Contractor).

Fluctuations – work sublet

A3·1 If the Contractor shall decide to sublet any portion of the Works, he shall incorporate in the sub-contract provisions to the like effect as the provisions of

clauses A1, A4 and A5 including the percentage stated in clause 4·6 pursuant to clause A5

which are applicable for the purposes of this Agreement.

A3·2 If the price payable under such a sub-contract as aforesaid is decreased below or increased above the price in such sub-contract by reason of the operation of the said incorporated provisions, then the net amount of such decrease or increase shall, as the case may be, be allowed by or paid to the Contractor under this Agreement.

Provisions relating to clauses A1, A2, A3 and A5

Written notice by Contractor

A4·1 The Contractor shall give a written notice to the Architect/the Contract Administrator of the occurrence of any of the events referred to in such of the following provisions as are applicable for the purposes of this Agreement:
·1 clause A1·2
·2 clause A1·6
·3 clause A2·2
·4 clause A3·2

Timing and effect of written notices

A4·2 Any notice required to be given by the preceding sub-clause shall be given within a reasonable time after the occurrence of the event to which the notice relates, and the giving of a written notice in that time shall be a condition precedent to any payment being made to the Contractor in respect of the event in question.

Agreement – Architect/Contract Administrator and Contractor

A4·3 The Architect/The Contract Administrator and the Contractor may agree what shall be deemed for all the purposes of this Agreement to be the net amount payable to or allowable by the Contractor in respect of the occurrence of any event such as is referred to in any of the provisions listed in clause A4·1.

Fluctuations added to or deducted from Contract Sum – provisions setting out conditions etc. to be fulfilled before such addition or deduction

A4·4 Any amount which from time to time becomes payable to or allowable by the Contractor by virtue of clause A1 or clause A3 shall, as the case may be, be added to or deducted from the Contract Sum:

Provided:

– evidence by Contractor –
·1 As soon as is reasonably practicable the Contractor shall provide such evidence as the Architect/the Contract Administrator may reasonably require to enable the amount payable to or allowable by the Contractor by virtue of clause A1 or clause A3 to be ascertained; and in the case of amounts payable to or allowable by the sub-contractor under clause A4·1·3 (or clause A3 for amounts payable to or allowable by the sub-contractor under provisions in the sub-contract to the like effect as clauses A1·3 and A1·4) – employees other than workpeople – such evidence shall include a certificate signed by or on behalf of the Contractor each week certifying the validity of the evidence reasonably required to ascertain such amounts.

– actual payment by Contractor –
·2 No amount shall be included in or deducted from the amount which would otherwise be stated as due in progress payments by virtue of this clause unless on or before the date as at which the total value of work, materials and goods is ascertained for the purposes of any progress payment the Contractor shall have actually paid or received the sum which is payable by or to him in consequence of the event in respect of which the payment or allowance arises.

– no alteration to Contractor's profit –
·3 No addition to or subtraction from the Contract Sum made by virtue of this clause shall alter in any way the amount of profit of the Contractor included in that Sum.

– position where Contractor in default over completion –
·4·1 No amount shall be included in or deducted from the amount which would otherwise be stated as due in progress payments or in the final certificate in respect of amounts otherwise payable to or allowable by the Contractor by virtue of clause A1 or clause A3 if the event (as referred to in the provisions listed in clause A4·1) in respect of which the payment or allowance would be made occurs after the completion date fixed under clause 2.

·4·2 Clause A4·4·4·1 shall not operate unless:
·1 the printed text of clause 2 is unamended; and
·2 the Architect/the Contract Administrator has, in respect of every written notification by the Contractor under clause 2 of this Agreement, fixed such completion date as he considered to be in accordance with that clause.

---

[w] See clause A4·6.

Work etc. to which clauses A1 and A3 not applicable
A4·5 Clause A1 and clause A3 shall not apply in respect of:

·1 work for which the Contractor is allowed daywork rates in accordance with any such rates included in the Contract Documents;

·2 changes in the rate of value added tax charged on the supply of goods or services by the Contractor to the Employer under this Agreement.

Definitions for use with clauses A1 and A2
A4·6 In clauses A1 and A2:

·1 the expression 'the date of tender' means the date 10 days before the date of this Agreement;

·2 the expressions 'materials' and 'goods' include timber used in formwork but do not include other consumable stores, plant and machinery;

·3 the expression 'workpeople' means persons whose rates of wages and other emoluments (including holiday credits) are governed by the rules or decisions or agreements of the Construction Industry Joint Council or some other wage-fixing body for trades associated with the building industry;

·4 the expression 'wage-fixing body' means a body which lays down recognised terms and conditions of workers within the meaning of the Employment Protection Act 1975, Schedule II, paragraph 2(a).

Percentage addition to fluctuation payments or allowances

A5 There shall be added to the amount paid to or allowed by the Contractor under:
·1 clause A1·2
·2 clause A1·3
·3 clause A1·6
·4 clause A2·2
·5 clause A3·2
the percentage stated in clause 4·6.

B: VALUE ADDED TAX
Clause 5·2

B1 In this Supplemental Condition B, 'VAT' means the value added tax introduced by the Finance Act 1972 which is under the care and management of the Commissioners of Customs and Excise (hereinafter called 'the Commissioners').

B1·1 ·1 Where in clause 5·2 it is stated that clause B1·1 applies, clauses B2·1 and B2·2 hereof shall not apply unless and until any notice issued under clause B1·1·4 hereof becomes effective or unless the Contractor fails to give the written notice required under clause B1·1·2. Where clause B1·1 applies clauses B1 and B3·1 to B10 inclusive remain in full force and effect.

·2 Not later than 7 days before the date for the issue of the first certificate under clause 4·2 the Contractor shall give written notice to the Employer, with a copy to the Architect/the Contract Administrator, of the rate of tax chargeable on the supply of goods and services for which certificates under clauses 4·2 and 4·3 and the final certificate under clause 4·5 are to be issued. If the rate of tax so notified is varied under statute the Contractor shall, not later than 7 days after the date when such varied rate comes into effect, send to the Employer, with a copy to the Architect/the Contract Administrator, the necessary amendment to the rate given in his written notice and that notice shall then take effect as so amended.

·3 For the purpose of complying with clause 5·2 for the payment by the Employer to the Contractor of tax properly chargeable by the Commissioners on the Contractor, an amount calculated at the rate given in the aforesaid written notice (or, where relevant, amended written notice) shall be shown on each certificate issued by the Architect/the Contract Administrator under clauses 4·2 and 4·3 and, unless the procedure set out in clause B3 hereof shall have been completed, on the final certificate issued by the Architect/the Contract Administrator under clause 4·5. Such amount shall be paid by the Employer to the Contractor or by the Contractor to the Employer as the case may be within the period for payment of certificates given in clauses 4·2, 4·3 and 4·5.

·4 Either the Employer or the Contractor may give written notice to the other, with a copy to the Architect/the Contract Administrator, stating that with effect from the date of the notice clause B1·1 shall no longer apply. From that date the provisions of clauses B2·1 and B2·2 shall apply in place of clause B1·1 hereof.

B2·1 Unless clause B1·1 applies, the Architect/the Contract Administrator shall inform the Contractor of the amount certified under clause 4·2 and immediately the Contractor shall give to the Employer a written provisional assessment of the respective values of those supplies of goods and services for which the certificate is being issued and which will be chargeable at the relevant times of supply on the Contractor at any rate or rates of VAT (including zero). The Contractor shall also specify the rate or rates of VAT which are chargeable on those supplies.

B2·2 Upon receipt of the Contractor's written provisional assessment the Employer shall calculate the amount of VAT due by applying the rate or rates of VAT specified by the Contractor to the amount of the supplies included in his assessment, and shall remit the calculated amount of such VAT to the Contractor when making payment to him of the amount certified by the Architect/the Contract Administrator under clause 4·2.

B3·1 Where clause B1·1 is operated, clause B3 only applies if no amount of tax pursuant to clause B1·1·3 has been shown on the final certificate issued by the Architect/the Contract Administrator. After the issue by the Architect/the

Contract Administrator of his certificate of making good defects under clause 2·5 of this Agreement the Contractor shall, as soon as he can finally so ascertain, prepare and submit to the Employer a written final statement of the value of all supplies of goods and services for which certificates have been or will be issued which are chargeable on the Contractor at any rate or rates of VAT (including zero). The Contractor shall also specify the rate or rates of VAT which are chargeable on those supplies and shall state the grounds on which he considers such supplies are so chargeable. He shall also state the total amount of VAT already received by him.

B3·2 Upon receipt of the written final statement the Employer shall calculate the amount of VAT due by applying the rate or rates of VAT specified by the Contractor to the value of the supplies included in the statement and deducting therefrom the total amount of VAT already received by the Contractor and shall pay the balance of such VAT to the Contractor within 28 days from receipt of the statement.

B3·3 If the Employer finds that the total amount of VAT specified in the final statement as already paid by him exceeds the amount of VAT calculated under clause B3·2, he shall so notify the Contractor, who shall refund such excess to the Employer within 28 days of receipt of the notification together with a receipt under clause B4 hereof showing a correction of the amounts for which a receipt or receipts have previously been issued by the Contractor.

B4 Upon receipt of any VAT properly paid under the provisions of this Supplemental Condition B the Contractor shall issue to the Employer an authenticated receipt of the kind referred to in Regulation 13(4) of the Value Added Tax Regulations 1995 or any amendment or re-enactment thereof.

B5·1 In calculating the amount of VAT to be paid to the Contractor under clauses B2 and B3 hereof, the Employer shall disregard any sums which the Contractor may be liable to pay or allow to the Employer, or which the Employer may deduct, under clause 2·3 as liquidated damages.

B5·2 The Contractor shall likewise disregard such liquidated damages when stating the value of supplies of goods or services in his written final statement under clause B3·1.

B5·3 Where clause B1·1 is operated the Employer shall pay the tax to which that clause refers notwithstanding any deduction which the Employer may be empowered to make by clause 2·3 from monies due to the Contractor under certificates for payment issued by the Architect/the Contract Administrator.

B6·1 If the Employer disagrees with the final statement issued by the Contractor under clause B3·1 he may request the Contractor to obtain the decision of the Commissioners on the VAT properly chargeable on the Contractor for all supplies of goods and services under this Agreement and the Contractor shall forthwith request the Commissioners for such decision.

B6·2 If the Employer disagrees with such decision, then, provided he secures the Contractor against all costs and other expenses, the Contractor shall in accordance with the instructions of the Employer make all such appeals against the decision of the Commissioners as the Employer may request.

B6·3 Within 28 days of the date of the decision of the Commissioners (or of the final adjudication of an appeal) the Employer or the Contractor, as the case may be, shall pay or refund to the other any VAT underpaid or overpaid in accordance with such decision or adjudication. The Contractor shall also account to the Employer for any costs awarded in his favour. The provisions of clause B3·3 shall apply in regard to the provision of authenticated receipts.

B7 The provisions of article 7A (*arbitration*) shall not apply to any matters to be dealt with under clause B6.

B8 If any dispute or difference between the Employer and the Contractor is referred for decision under the procedures under this Agreement relevant to the resolution of disputes or differences, then, in so far as any payment awarded by such decision varies amounts certified for payment of goods or services supplied by the Contractor to the Employer under this Agreement or is an amount which ought to have been but was not so certified, the provisions of this Supplemental Condition B shall so far as relevant and applicable apply to any such payments.

B9 Notwithstanding any provisions to the contrary elsewhere in this Agreement the Employer shall not be obliged to make any further payment to the Contractor if the Contractor is in default in providing the receipt referred to in clause B4; provided that this clause B9 shall only apply where

the Employer can show that he requires such receipt to validate any claim for credit for tax paid or payable under this Supplemental Condition B which the Employer is entitled to make to the Commissioners and

the Employer has paid tax in accordance with the provisional assessment of the Contractor under clause B2·2 or paid tax in accordance with clause B1·1.

B10 The Employer shall be discharged from any further liability to pay tax to the Contractor under the clause upon payment of tax in accordance either with clause B3·2 (adjusted where relevant in accordance with the decision in any appeal to which clause B6 refers) or with clause B1·1·3 in respect of the tax shown in the final certificate. Provided always that if after the due discharge under clause B10 the Commissioners decide to correct the tax due from the Contractor on the supply to the Employer of any goods and services by the Contractor under this Agreement the amount of such correction shall be an additional payment by the Employer to the Contractor or by the Contractor to the Employer as the case may be. The provisions of clause B6 in regard to disagreement with any decision of the Commissioners shall apply to any decision referred to in this proviso.

C: CONSTRUCTION INDUSTRY SCHEME (CIS) [x]
Clause 5·3

Definitions

C1 In this Supplemental Condition C:

'the Act' means the Income and Corporation Taxes Act 1988 or any statutory amendment or modification thereof;

'Authorisation' means:

either 'CIS 4', the registration card designated 'CIS 4(T)' and which has an expiry date or 'CIS 4(P)', in the form provided by regulations 7 and 7C of the Regulations appearing as shown in Schedule 1 of the Regulations and issued by the Inland Revenue;

or 'CIS 5' or 'CIS 6', the certificates in the form provided by regulation 24 of the Regulations and appearing as shown in Schedule 1 of the Regulations and issued by the Inland Revenue;

or a 'certifying document' created on the Contractor's letter headed stationery, not a fax or photocopy, in the form prescribed by regulation 34 of the Regulations;

'construction operations' means those operations defined in S.567 of the Act as construction operations;

'contractor' means a person who is a contractor for the purposes of the Act and the Regulations;

'the direct cost of materials' means the direct cost to the Contractor or to any other person of materials used or to be used in carrying out the construction operations to which the contract under which the payment is made relates as provided in regulation 7 of the Regulations;

'the Regulations' means the Income Tax (Sub-Contractors in the Construction Industry) Regulations 1993 S.I. No. 743 as amended by the Income Tax (Sub-Contractors in the Construction Industry) (Amendment) Regulations 1998 S.I. No. 2622 or any amendment or re-making thereof;

'statutory deduction' means the deduction which is in force at the time of payment referred to in S.559(4) and (4A) of the Act;

'sub-contractor' means a person who is a sub-contractor for the purposes of the Act and the Regulations;

'voucher' means:

either a tax payment voucher in the form CIS 25 provided by regulation 7 and appearing as shown in Schedule 1 of the Regulations and issued by the Inland Revenue;

or a gross payment voucher CIS 24 in the form provided by regulation 29 and appearing as shown in Schedule 1 of the Regulations and issued by the Inland Revenue.

Whether Employer is a 'contractor'

C2 Where the Employer is not a 'contractor' clauses C3 to C14 shall not apply. Nevertheless if, at any time up to the payment of the final certificate, the Employer becomes such a 'contractor', the Employer shall so inform the Contractor and the provisions of clauses C3 to C14 shall thereupon become operative.

---

[x] The application of the Construction Industry Scheme (CIS) and these provisions is explained in JCT Practice Note 1 (Series 2).

Payment by Employer – valid Authorisation essential

C3 The Employer shall not make any payment under or pursuant to this Agreement unless a valid Authorisation has been provided to him or his nominated representative by the Contractor.

Validity of Authorisation – Employer's query

C4·1 If the Employer or his nominated representative is not satisfied with the validity of the Authorisation provided by the Contractor, he shall thereupon notify the Contractor in writing of his grounds for considering that the Authorisation is not valid.

C4·2 Where a notification has been given under clause C4·1, the Employer shall not make any payment under or pursuant to this Agreement until

either the Employer or his nominated representative has received an Authorisation which he considers to be valid

or the Contractor has re-submitted the Authorisation with a letter from the Contractor's tax office, confirming that that Authorisation is valid.

Authorisation: CIS 4 registration card

C5·1 Where the Authorisation is a CIS 4 registration card, then 7 days before the final date for payment of any sum due:

·1 the Contractor shall give to the Employer a statement showing the direct cost of materials to the Contractor and to any other persons to be included in the payment; and

·2 the Employer shall make the statutory deduction from that part of the payment which is not in respect of the direct cost of materials as stated by the Contractor pursuant to clause C5·1·1.

C5·2 Where the Contractor complies with clause C5·1·1 he shall indemnify the Employer against any loss or expense caused to the Employer by any incorrect statement of the amount of direct cost referred to in clause C5·1·1.

C5·3 Where the Contractor fails to comply with clause C5·1·1, or where the Employer has reasonable grounds to believe that any statement provided in compliance with clause C5·1·1 is incorrect, the Employer shall make a fair estimate of the direct cost of materials.

Authorisation: CIS 5 or CIS 6 or a certifying document

C6 Where the Authorisation is a valid CIS 5 or CIS 6 or a certifying document the Employer shall pay any amount due without making the statutory deduction.

Change of Authorisation

C7 Where the Authorisation is a CIS 4 but the Contractor is subsequently issued with a CIS 5 or CIS 6 by the Inland Revenue, the Contractor shall immediately inform the Employer and either present the CIS 5 or CIS 6 in person to the Employer or his nominated representative or send to the Employer or his nominated representative a certifying document. Provided the Employer or his nominated representative is satisfied with the validity of the changed Authorisation, clause C6 shall thereupon apply.

C8 If an Authorisation CIS 5 or CIS 6 is withdrawn by the Inland Revenue for any reason, the Contractor shall thereupon notify the Employer or his authorised representative and the Employer shall make no further payments to the Contractor under or pursuant to this Agreement until the Contractor provides the Employer or his authorised representative with a valid Authorisation CIS 4. After such provision clauses C5·1, C5·2 and C5·3 shall apply.

C9   If an Authorisation CIS 5 or CIS 6 expires, the Employer shall make no further payments to the Contractor under or pursuant to this Agreement until the Contractor:

either   shows in person to the Employer or his nominated representative an Authorisation CIS 4 and if so clauses C5·1, C5·2 and C5·3 shall apply;

or   provides to the Employer or his nominated representative an Authorisation CIS 5 or CIS 6 or a certifying document and if so clause C6 shall apply.

Vouchers
C10   Where Authorisation CIS 4 applies and the Employer has made payments to the Contractor, the Employer shall within 14 days of the end of the income tax month [x·1] in which the payment is made provide the Contractor with a copy of the CIS 25 voucher that he has sent to the Inland Revenue showing all the payments made in the tax month concerned and the total tax deducted.

C11   Where Authorisation CIS 6 applies and the Employer has made payments to the Contractor, the Contractor shall within 14 days of the end of the income tax month [x·1] in which the payment is made provide the CIS 24 voucher to the Employer who shall add thereto his tax reference and send the voucher to the Inland Revenue with a copy to the Contractor.

Correction of errors in making the statutory deduction
C12   Where the Employer has made an error or omission in calculating the statutory deduction, he may correct the error by repayment or further deduction from payments due to the Contractor, subject only to an instruction by the Inland Revenue to the Employer not to make such a correction.

Relation to other clauses
C13   If compliance with this Supplemental Condition C involves the Employer or the Contractor in not complying with any other of the Conditions, then the provisions of this Supplemental Condition C shall prevail.

Disputes or differences
C14   The relevant procedures applicable under this Agreement to the resolution of disputes or differences between the Employer and the Contractor shall apply to any dispute or difference between the Employer and the Contractor as to the operation of this Supplemental Condition C except where the Act or the Regulations or any other Act of Parliament or statutory instrument, rule or order made under any Act of Parliament provide for some other method of resolving such dispute or difference.

[x·1]   The income tax month ends on the 5th day of the month.

D: ADJUDICATION
Clause 8·1

Application of Supplemental Condition D
D1   Supplemental Condition D applies where, pursuant to article 6, either party (i.e. the Employer or the Contractor) refers any dispute or difference arising under this Agreement to adjudication.

Identity of Adjudicator
D2   The Adjudicator to decide the dispute or difference shall be either an individual agreed by the parties or, on the application of either party, an individual to be nominated as the Adjudicator by the person named in article 6 ('the nominator') [y]. Provided that

D2·1   no Adjudicator shall be agreed or nominated under clause D2·2 or clause D3 who will not execute the Standard Agreement for the appointment of an Adjudicator issued by the JCT (the 'JCT Adjudication Agreement' [z]) with the parties [y], and

D2·2   where either party has given notice of his intention to refer a dispute to adjudication then

  – any agreement by the parties on the appointment of an Adjudicator must be reached with the object of securing the appointment of, and the referral of the dispute or difference to, the Adjudicator within 7 days of the date of the notice of intention to refer (see clause D4·1);

  – any application to the nominator must be made with the object of securing the appointment of, and the referral of the dispute or difference to, the Adjudicator within 7 days of the date of the notice of intention to refer.

Upon agreement by the parties on the appointment of the Adjudicator or upon receipt by the parties from the nominator of the name of the nominated Adjudicator the parties shall thereupon execute with the Adjudicator the JCT Adjudication Agreement.

Death of Adjudicator – inability to adjudicate
D3   If the Adjudicator dies or becomes ill or is unavailable for some other cause and is thus unable to adjudicate on a dispute or difference referred to him, then either the parties may agree upon an individual to replace the Adjudicator or either party may apply to the nominator for the nomination of an adjudicator to adjudicate that dispute or difference; and the parties shall execute the JCT Adjudication Agreement with the agreed or nominated Adjudicator.

Dispute or difference – notice of intention to refer to adjudication – referral
D4·1   When pursuant to article 6 a party requires a dispute or difference to be referred to adjudication then that party shall give notice to the other party of his intention to refer the dispute or difference, briefly identified in the notice, to adjudication. If an Adjudicator is agreed or appointed

---

[y]   The nominators named in article 6 have agreed with the JCT that they will comply with the requirements of Supplemental Condition D on the nomination of an adjudicator including the requirement in clause D2·2 for the nomination to be made with the object of securing the appointment of, and the referral of the dispute or difference to, the Adjudicator within 7 days of the date of the notice of intention to refer; and will only nominate adjudicators who will enter into the 'JCT Adjudication Agreement'.

[z]   The JCT Adjudication Agreement is available from the retailers of JCT Forms.
A version of this Agreement is also available for use if the parties have named an Adjudicator in their agreement.

within 7 days of the notice then the party giving the notice shall refer the dispute or difference to the Adjudicator ('the referral') within 7 days of the notice. If an Adjudicator is not agreed or appointed within 7 days of the notice the referral shall be made immediately on such agreement or appointment. The said party shall include with that referral particulars of the dispute or difference together with a summary of the contentions on which he relies, a statement of the relief or remedy which is sought and any material he wishes the Adjudicator to consider. The referral and its accompanying documentation shall be copied simultaneously to the other party.

D4·2 The referral by a party with its accompanying documentation to the Adjudicator and the copies thereof to be provided to the other party shall be given by actual delivery or by FAX or by special delivery or recorded delivery. If given by FAX then, for record purposes, the referral and its accompanying documentation must forthwith be sent by first class post or given by actual delivery. If sent by special delivery or recorded delivery the referral and its accompanying documentation shall, subject to proof to the contrary, be deemed to have been received 48 hours after the date of posting subject to the exclusion of Sundays and any Public Holiday.

Conduct of the adjudication

D5·1 The Adjudicator shall immediately upon receipt of the referral and its accompanying documentation confirm that receipt to the parties.

D5·2 The party not making the referral may, by the same means stated in clause D4·2, send to the Adjudicator within 7 days of the date of the referral, with a copy to the other party, a written statement of the contentions on which he relies and any material he wishes the Adjudicator to consider.

D5·3 The Adjudicator shall within 28 days of the referral under clause D4·1, and acting as an Adjudicator for the purposes of S.108 of the Housing Grants, Construction and Regeneration Act 1996 and not as an expert or an arbitrator, reach his decision and forthwith send that decision in writing to the parties. Provided that the party who has made the referral may consent to allowing the Adjudicator to extend the period of 28 days by up to 14 days; and that by agreement between the parties after the referral has been made a longer period than 28 days may be notified jointly by the parties to the Adjudicator within which to reach his decision.

D5·4 The Adjudicator shall not be obliged to give reasons for his decision.

D5·5 In reaching his decision the Adjudicator shall act impartially and set his own procedure; and at his absolute discretion may take the initiative in ascertaining the facts and the law as he considers necessary in respect of the referral which may include the following:

·1 using his own knowledge and/or experience;

·2 opening up, reviewing and revising any certificate, opinion, decision, requirement or notice issued, given or made under this Agreement as if no such certificate, opinion, decision, requirement or notice had been issued, given or made;

·3 requiring from the parties further information than that contained in the notice of referral and its accompanying documentation or in any written statement provided by the parties including the results of any tests that have been made or of any opening up;

·4 requiring the parties to carry out tests or additional tests or to open up work or further open up work;

·5 visiting the site of the Works or any workshop where work is being or has been prepared for this Agreement;

·6 obtaining such information as he considers necessary from any employee or representative of the parties provided that before obtaining information from an employee of a party he has given prior notice to that party;

·7 obtaining from others such information and advice as he considers necessary on technical and on legal matters subject to giving prior notice to the parties together with a statement or estimate of the cost involved;

·8 having regard to any term of this Agreement relating to the payment of interest, deciding the circumstance in which or the period for which a simple rate of interest shall be paid.

D5·6 Any failure by either party to enter into the JCT Adjudication Agreement or to comply with any requirement of the Adjudicator under clause D5·5 or with any provision in or requirement under Supplemental Condition D shall not invalidate the decision of the Adjudicator.

D5·7 The parties shall meet their own costs of the adjudication except that the Adjudicator may direct as to who should pay the cost of any test or opening up if required pursuant to clause D5·5·4.

Adjudicator's fee and reasonable expenses – payment

D6·1 The Adjudicator in his decision shall state how payment of his fee and reasonable expenses is to be apportioned as between the parties. In default of such statement the parties shall bear the cost of the Adjudicator's fee and reasonable expenses in equal proportions.

D6·2 The parties shall be jointly and severally liable to the Adjudicator for his fee and for all expenses reasonably incurred by the Adjudicator pursuant to the adjudication.

Effect of Adjudicator's decision

D7·1 The decision of the Adjudicator shall be binding on the parties until the dispute or difference is finally determined by arbitration or by legal proceedings or by an agreement in writing between the parties made after the decision of the Adjudicator has been given. [aa]

D7·2 The parties shall, without prejudice to their other rights under this Agreement, comply with the decision of the Adjudicator; and the Employer and the Contractor shall ensure that the decision of the Adjudicator is given effect.

D7·3 If either party does not comply with the decision of the Adjudicator the other party shall be entitled to take legal proceedings to secure such compliance pending any final determination of the referred dispute or difference pursuant to clause D7·1.

Immunity

D8 The Adjudicator shall not be liable for anything done or omitted in the discharge or purported discharge of his functions as Adjudicator unless the act or omission is in bad faith and this protection from liability shall similarly extend to any employee or agent of the Adjudicator.

[aa] The arbitration or legal proceedings are not an appeal against the decision of the Adjudicator but are a consideration of the dispute or difference as if no decision had been made by an Adjudicator.

E: ARBITRATION
Clause 8·2

E1 Any reference in Supplemental Condition E to a Rule or Rules is a reference to the JCT 1998 edition of the Construction Industry Model Arbitration Rules (CIMAR) current at the date of this Agreement.

E2·1 Where pursuant to article 7A either party requires a dispute or difference to be referred to arbitration then that party shall serve on the other party a notice of arbitration to such effect in accordance with Rule 2.1 which states:

> "Arbitral proceedings are begun in respect of a dispute when one party serves on the other a written notice of arbitration identifying the dispute and requiring him to agree to the appointment of an arbitrator";

and an arbitrator shall be an individual agreed by the parties or appointed by the person named in article 7A in accordance with Rule 2.3 which states:

> "If the parties fail to agree on the name of an arbitrator within 14 days (or any agreed extension) after:
> (i) the notice of arbitration is served, or
> (ii) a previously appointed arbitrator ceases to hold office for any reason,
> either party may apply for the appointment of an arbitrator to the person so empowered."

By Rule 2.5:

> "the arbitrator's appointment takes effect upon his agreement to act or his appointment under Rule 2.3, whether or not his terms have been accepted."

E2·2 Where two or more related arbitral proceedings in respect of the Works fall under separate arbitration agreements, Rules 2.6, 2.7 and 2.8 shall apply thereto.

E2·3 After an arbitrator has been appointed either party may give a further notice of arbitration to the other party and to the Arbitrator referring any other dispute which falls under article 7A to be decided in the arbitral proceedings and Rule 3.3 shall apply thereto.

E3 Subject to the provisions of article 7A the Arbitrator shall, without prejudice to the generality of his powers, have power to rectify this Agreement so that it accurately reflects the true agreement made by the parties, to direct such measurements and/or valuations as may in his opinion be desirable in order to determine the rights of the parties and to ascertain and award any sum which ought to have been the subject of or included in any certificate and to open up, review and revise any certificate, opinion, decision, requirement or notice and to determine all matters in dispute which shall be submitted to him in the same manner as if no such certificate, opinion, decision, requirement or notice had been given.

E4 Subject to clause E5 the award of such Arbitrator shall be final and binding on the parties.

E5 The parties hereby agree pursuant to S.45(2)(a) and S.69(2)(a) of the Arbitration Act 1996 that either party may (upon notice to the other party and to the Arbitrator):

·1 apply to the courts to determine any question of law arising in the course of the reference; and

·2 appeal to the courts on any question of law arising out of an award made in an arbitration under this Agreement.

E6 The provisions of the Arbitration Act 1996 shall apply to any arbitration under this Agreement wherever the same, or any part of it, shall be conducted. [bb]

E7 The arbitration shall be conducted in accordance with the JCT 1998 edition of the Construction Industry Model Arbitration Rules (CIMAR) current at the date of this Agreement. Provided that if any amendments to the Rules so current at the date of this Agreement have been issued by the JCT after the date of this Agreement the parties may, by a joint notice in writing to the Arbitrator, state that they wish the arbitration to be conducted in accordance with the Rules as so amended.

[bb] It should be noted that the provisions of the Arbitration Act 1996 do not extend to Scotland. Where the site of the Works is situated in Scotland then the forms issued by the Scottish Building Contract Committee which contain Scots proper law and adjudication and arbitration provisions are the appropriate documents. The SBCC issues guidance in this respect.

Guidance Note

Use of Agreement for Minor Building Works

1. The Agreement should *only* be used between a building contractor and a *client who has engaged an architect or some other professionally qualified person to advise on and to administer its terms.*

2. The Form of Agreement and Conditions are designed for use:
   - where minor building works are to be carried out for an agreed lump sum; and
   - the work involved is simple in character.

3. The Agreement is predicated upon the lump sum offer obtained being based on drawings and/or a specification and/or schedules but without detailed measurements. Those documents should therefore be in a form sufficient to enable the Contractor accurately to identify the Works to be done without the provision of bills of quantities by the Employer.

4. This Agreement is not suitable for use where the Works are of a complex nature such that bills of quantities would ordinarily be necessary or where the period required for the execution of the Works is such that full labour and materials fluctuation provisions are required.

5. For Works which do not fulfil the criteria mentioned above, reference should be made to JCT Practice Note 5 (Series 2) for guidance as to the appropriate contract to be used.

6. The Contractor should be informed whether the Employer is or becomes a 'contractor' for the purposes of the Construction Industry Scheme (CIS) to which Supplemental Condition C refers; if he is a 'contractor' then Supplemental Condition C will apply and the Contractor must satisfy its provisions, in particular on providing evidence that the Employer may make payments without being required to make the statutory deduction.

7. In some contracts where there is an intention to use the Agreement, the Employer may wish to seek to control the selection of subcontractors for specialist work. This may be done by naming a person or company in the tender documents or in instructions on the expenditure of a provisional sum but there are no provisions in the Agreement which deal with the consequences of such naming; nor is there any standard form of subcontract which would be applicable to such selected subcontractors. Such control of selection may be better achieved by the Employer entering into a direct contract with the specialist.

Outline of the Agreement

Parties

8. These are the client (referred to as 'the Employer') and the building contractor (referred to as 'the Contractor').

Employer's professional agent

9. This is the person whom the client has engaged to advise on and administer the Agreement. If the Employer engages a professional agent who is not an architect, that person is referred to in the Agreement as the 'Contract Administrator'. Whether the professional agent is an 'Architect' or a 'Contract Administrator', his/her duties under the Agreement are the same.

Role of the Architect/Contract Administrator

10. The Architect/Contract Administrator is paid by the Employer and advises the Employer on all matters in connection with the building work and administers the Agreement on behalf of the Employer; however in the following matters he/she acts independently as between the Employer and the Contractor:

    - in issuing all payment certificates;

    - in valuing any Variations or any work instructed in respect of provisional sums (see "Terms used") included in the Contract Documents;

    - in making any extension to the time stated in the Agreement for the completion of the building work;

    - in certifying the date of practical completion (see "Terms used") and the date when in his opinion all defects which appear during the defects liability period (see "Terms used") have been made good.

Instructions

11. Under the Agreement only the Architect/Contract Administrator can issue instructions to the Contractor; although the Employer is paying for the building work he is not entitled to give any instructions direct to the Contractor in connection therewith; if the Employer wishes to make any change to the work or the manner in which it is being carried out he must ask the Architect/Contract Administrator to give the necessary instructions to the Contractor.

Price

12. This is the lump sum stated in the Agreement plus any VAT properly chargeable on the building work. This lump sum may be increased or decreased depending on any changes to the work (Variations) or the value of work in respect of provisional sums included in the Contract Documents as may be instructed by the Architect/Contract Administrator.

Payment

13 .1 Payment is made under certificates issued by the Architect/Contract Administrator every 4 weeks calculated from the date of commencement until practical completion. A further certificate is issued within 14 days of practical completion. The final balance is paid following the issue of the final certificate. The final date for payment of certificates together with any VAT chargeable to the Employer is 14 days from the date of the issue of the certificate.

.2 Certificates will reflect the fact that the Employer is entitled to withhold a percentage of 5% (or any different percentage stated in the Agreement) from amounts due to the Contractor up until practical completion. Between practical completion and the final certificate, the percentage is halved.

.3 If the Employer fails to pay an amount due to the Contractor by the final date for its payment, interest at 5% over the Bank of England Base Rate is payable by the Employer for the period until such payment is made.

Time-scale for the work

14 .1 If the work cannot be finished within the original time stated in the Agreement for reasons beyond the control of the Contractor, the Architect/Contract Administrator shall give an extension of time.

.2 The Employer can recover liquidated damages (see "Terms used") from the Contractor if the work is not finished by the Completion Date (see "Terms used") having taken into account any extension of time.

Suspension of work

15 If the Employer does not pay the amount due to the Contractor by the final date for its payment, the Contractor can, after giving notice, suspend performance of his obligations under the Agreement until payment of that amount is made.

Termination

16 Either party may end the Contractor's employment if the other does not comply with certain stated obligations or if one of the parties becomes insolvent.

Dealing with disputes

17 Disputes are dealt with either by arbitration or through the courts depending on which option is stated in the Agreement. Either party may also refer any dispute for a "fast track" decision by an adjudicator; such decision is binding unless and until the dispute is reheard and decided by an arbitrator or the court as if no adjudication had taken place.

Rights and remedies generally

18 Statutory and common law rights are not restricted by the terms of the Agreement. Proceedings can be commenced within 6 years from the date of the breach if the Agreement is simply signed by the parties, or 12 years if it is signed as a deed or is under seal.

Terms used

19 The Architect/Contract Administrator should, as part of his/her duties to the Employer, be prepared to explain the general meanings of the various terms used in the Agreement. For example:

Assignment

20 The transfer of rights under the Agreement by one party to a third person. For example, the Contractor may transfer (assign) his rights to payment to 'X'. The Employer will then be required to pay 'X' instead of the Contractor.

CDM Regulations

21 Regulations made by Act of Parliament to improve health and safety standards on construction sites.

Completion date

22 The date by which the Contractor is required to finish the work.

Date of practical completion

23 The date certified by the Architect/Contract Administrator when in his opinion the Contractor actually finishes the work to all practical intents and purposes except for minor matters which the Contractor puts right during the defects liability period.

Defects liability period

24 The time period (three months from the date of practical completion unless otherwise agreed) during which defects in the work which appear during that time period are required to be put right by the Contractor before he is entitled to be paid the balance of the monies due to him under the Agreement.

Health and safety file

25 A manual which the Planning Supervisor has to ensure is delivered to the Employer on completion of the work, giving information for the future on the management of health and safety in the maintenance, repair, renovation, occupancy or demolition of the work and its contents. It is only required where the CDM Regulations apply in full (they do not apply in full to private householders having work done on their own premises).

Insurance in the joint names

26 A policy of insurance under which both parties are covered if certain events occur.

27   Each party should obtain advice from his own insurers about coverage of the risks stated in the Agreement. *This should be done before the Agreement is signed.* The Agreement does not require that the insurance in the joint names of the Employer and the Contractor in respect of the work should cover theft, vandalism or impact and the advice obtained should deal with any necessary cover for these risks. Employers who are domestic householders should, in any event, notify their Building and Contents insurers that they will be having building work done so that any temporary modifications to their policies can be put into effect.

28   Any excesses under a policy are normally borne by the party required to take out the insurance.

Liquidated damages

29   The rate per day/week/month stated *in the Agreement* by the Employer, to compensate him for the Contractor's failure to finish the work on time. The rate should be a genuine pre-estimate by the Employer of the financial loss that he is likely to suffer. It is for the Employer to decide if he is entitled to deduct liquidated damages from any amount certified as due to the Contractor; such deduction is not taken into account by the Architect/Contract Administrator in the calculation of any certificate.

Planning Supervisor

30   The person named as the Planning Supervisor in the Agreement or subsequently appointed as such as required by the CDM Regulations.

Provisional sum

31   A sum included for work which the Employer may or may not decide to have carried out, or which cannot be accurately specified in the original contract documents. For instance, the pricing documents may say "Allow £X for complete external redecoration of the premises." In the event, the Employer may decide to have all, some or none of the outside of the premises re-decorated. If redecoration is wanted by the Employer the specification required is instructed by the Architect/Contract Administrator; and the price to be paid is either agreed between the Employer and the Contractor or valued by the Architect/Contract Administrator.

Construction Industry Scheme (CIS)

32   A statutory framework for ensuring that Contractors and their sub-contractors comply with their obligations to the Inland Revenue. The CIS places an obligation on some Employers *(who for the purposes of the Scheme are treated as though they are 'contractors')* not to make any payment under a contract to a Contractor unless the Contractor has the necessary clearance from the Inland Revenue enabling him to be paid either in full or less a deduction laid down by statute. CIS does not affect Employers who are private householders having work done on their own premises. In all other cases Employers should seek advice from the Architect/Contract Administrator and, if there is any doubt, from the Inland Revenue.

Variation

33   A change to the work ordered by the Architect/Contract Administrator on behalf of the Employer. The Variation may be an addition to or an omission from the originally specified work.

While care has been taken in preparing this Guidance Note it should not be treated as a definitive legal interpretation or commentary. Users are reminded that the effect in law of the provisions of the Agreement for Minor Building Works 1998 Edition is, in the event of a dispute as to that effect, a matter for decision in adjudication, arbitration or litigation.

Agreement for Minor Building Works

This reprint incorporates the following amendments.

A **Amendment 1, June 1999**
Construction Industry Scheme (CIS)
(incorporated April 2000)

1. **Section 4**
   new clause 4A inserted
2. **clause 5·3**
   redrafted
3. **Supplemental Condition C**
   redrafted

B **Amendment 2, January 2000**
Sundry amendments
(incorporated April 2000)

1. **article 6**
   additional text inserted
2. **Section 1**
   new clause 1·8 inserted
3. **Supplemental Condition A**
   clause A2·1 amended
   clause A2·2 amended
   clause A2·3 deleted

   Consequential amendment
   clause A4·6·2

   Correction to Amendment 2 made and incorporated in reprint dated April 2000
   Clause A2·2
   footnote reference [w] inserted

C **Amendments and corrections made and incorporated in reprint dated April 2000**

1. **"Agreement" substituted for "Contract"**
   clause 2·3
   clause 4·3
   clause 5·1
   clause 7·2·1
2. **"Construction Industry Joint Council" substituted for "National Joint Council for the Building Industry"**
   clauses A1·4 and A4·6·3
3. **Corrections to clause number cross-references**
   clauses A3·1, A4·6 and A5
   clauses B1·1·2 and B1·1·3
   heading to Supplemental Condition E
4. **Minor corrections to wording, upper and lower case and punctuation**
   recitals 1, 5A and 5B
   articles 1, 4A, 4B, 5, 6 and 7A
   clause 1·2
   clause 3·6
   clauses 4·2·1 and 4·5·1·4
   clause 5·1
   clauses 6·1, 6·2, 6·3A and 6·3B
   clause 7·3·3
   clauses A1, A1·4, A2·2 and A4·3
   clauses B1 and B8
   clauses D1, D5·1, D5·6 and D5·7
   clause E5
5. **Practice Note/Guidance Note**
   Practice Note M2 deleted
   new Guidance Note inserted
   maximum value revised

D **Amendment 3, January 2001**
Construction Industry Scheme
(incorporated March 2001)

1. **Supplemental Condition C**
   clauses C10 and C11 amended
   footnote [x·1] inserted

E **Amendment 4, January 2002**
Dispute resolution/Defects liability/Progress payments/ Payment and deducation notices/ Attestation
(incorporated July 2002)

1. **Article 7**
   new clause 7C inserted
2. **Clause 2·5**
   amended
3. **Clauses 4·2**
   Clauses 4·2·1 and 4·2·2 amended
4. **Clause 4·4**
   clause 4·4·2 amended
5. **Attestation**
   for execution as a deed/under seal added

F **Corrections**
(incorporated July 2002)

1. **'Construction Industry Scheme substituted for 'statutory tax deducation scheme**
   article 7A
2. **Section 3**
   clause 3·6 renumbered as clause 3·7
   clause 3·7 renumbered as clause 3·8
3. **Section 4**
   clause 4·1 renumbered as clause 3·6
   clause 4·A renumbered as clause 4·1
4. **Section 5**
   footnote [v]: 2nd paragraph deleted
5. **Supplemental Condition A**
   reference to Finance Act deleted
6. **Supplemental Condition B**
   clause B4: references to Act and Regulations updated
7. **Guidance Note**
   paragraphs 2–10 amended
8. **Minor corrections to wording and punctuation**
   throughout contract

G **Amendment 5: July 2003**
Construction Skills Certification Scheme
(incorporated September 2003)

1. **Clause 1·1**
   clause 1·1 renumbered as clause 1·1·1
   new clause 1·1·2 inserted